Summer Rays

Also by Randah Ribhi Hamadeh (in Arabic):

Samar—Sunset and Sunrise
Samar, the Sun that Does Not Set

Summer Rays

Solace for Bereaved Parents

Randah Ribhi Hamadeh

iUniverse, Inc.
New York   Bloomington

Summer Rays
Solace for Bereaved Parents

iUniverse books may be ordered through booksellers or by contacting:

iUniverse
1663 Liberty Drive
Bloomington, IN 47403
www.iuniverse.com
1-800-Authors (1-800-288-4677)

Because of the dynamic nature of the Internet, any Web addresses or links contained in this book may have changed since publication and may no longer be valid.

ISBN: 978-1-4401-5160-6 (sc)
ISBN: 978-1-4401-5162-0 (dj)
ISBN: 978-1-4401-5161-3 (ebk)

Printed in the United States of America

iUniverse rev. date: 6/30/2009

To my precious daughter,

Samar Ahmed Al Ansari

(4/4/1988–4/9/2006)

with all my love

Samar

Contents

Foreword xi
Preface xv
Acknowledgments xix
SAMAR 1
Twenty -One 3
A Year Has Passed 5
Why Did You Come, 2008? 7
Eighteen Months 9
Mother's Day 11
It's So Unfair 13
Oh, September, You Came Back Again 15
Season's Greetings 17
2009 19
Eighteen Years 21
Oh, Days! 23
I'm So Sorry 25
I Wish 27
I Miss You 29
Why Did I Die? 31
You Are a Star 33
You Tumbled Short of Your Dreams 35
I Carry Her in My Heart 37
My Heart Is Broken 39
Days Are Not the Same 41
The Incomplete 43
Going to Places 45
Little Bo Peep 47
If You Had One More Day 49
Can You Take Away My Endless Pain? 51
Why Are You Not Moving On? 53
Don't Ask Me 55
How Many Children? 57

Men Can Cry 59
A Mother's Grief 61
You Will Heal 63
For Those I Left Behind 65
I Am Not Walking Alone 67
You and I. 69
Dear Nieces. 71
Thank You, Friend. 73
Could That Have Been You? 75
I Look for You. 77
Never Died 79
Hello from Heaven 81
Please, Mother, Don't Cry 83
My Most Dear. 85
You'll Find Me. 87
About the Author 89

Foreword
by Gloria Horsley

Randah Ribhi Hamadeh's *Summer Rays: Solace for Bereaved Parents* is a poetic diary of loss, and communication with the eternal soul. Through her poems, all bereaved parents, including me, will identify with the heartfelt pleadings of a grieving parent and the connection with her lost child. They will find her poetry profound as she describes the familiar excruciating pain of a grieving parent, in particular on the special occasions where the lost child is missed, like birthdays, anniversaries, Mother's Day and New Year's Day. They will also relate to her feelings of gratitude towards those who were supportive and frustration with those less understanding.

Some of the poems are poignantly written in the voice of Randah's deceased daughter, Samar, as in *"I wish," "My Most Dear," "Hello from* heaven," *"I'm so* sorry," and *"You'll Find* Me." In her poem *"My Most* Dear," Randah gives the inspiration for her poetry when she writes in the last stanza that *"although I am very far, I am so* near." She also displays it in the second stanza of *"Hello from* heaven*"* when Samar says, *"You'll feel my presence, no need to ask how or* why." Indeed, her deceased daughter, Samar, is only as distant as the poetic connection. In this, her third volume of poems and the first written in English, Randah writes with deep and spiritual feelings as she deals with grief, survival, and recovery.

Although not a poet, I am inspired by those who share their journey of loss, hope, and healing through poems and diaries. Writings from the soul are cathartic not only for the authors but for all who share their unthinkable sorrow. As with any writing, when the writer takes up the pen, the muse will appear. In this case, the muse is Samar Ahmed Al Ansari, the author's deceased daughter.

Randah, a professor at the Arabian Gulf University in Bahrain, had rarely written poetry, but after the death of her daughter, she took up the pen and followed her heart to a new challenge. Through this volume, she shows us that beauty and love can rise through the winter of our sadness and despair.

Gloria Horsley Ph.D.
Author of *In-laws: A Guide to Extended Family Therapy* (1996), *The In-Law Survival Manual: Cultivating Healthy In-Law Relationships (1997)*, *TEEN GRIEF RELIEF: Parenting with Understanding, Support and Guidance (2007)*
President of the Open to Hope Foundation
National Board Member of the Compassionate Friends
Host of the Radio Show *Healing the Grieving Heart*
Media spokesperson for the Compassionate Friends Grief Consultant
www.thegriefblog.com
www.opentohope.com

by Genesse Bourdeau Gentry

Randah Ribhi Hamadeh's poems in her book of poetry, *Summer Rays*, are cries from the soul, and the searingly honest expressions of her thoughts and feelings will be instantly recognizable to all bereaved parents. I loved the poems to and from her daughter, Samar, and to her own friends and acquaintances, the ones who can really be there for her and the ones who want her to move on. I also found "*How Many* Children?" to be particularly powerful. This book will truly give solace to bereaved parents, especially those in early grief.

Genesse Bourdeau Gentry
Author of *Stars in the Deepest Night* and *Catching the Light - Coming Back to Life after the Death of a Child (2009)*
Contributing author to: www.opentohope.com
Regional Coordinator for N. California, The Compassionate Friends (TCF) www.compassionatefriends.org
Steering Committee member of TCF Marin www.tcfmarin.org

Preface

I began writing poetry in Arabic exactly a month since the day that terrible car accident took our dearest Samar away from us on September 4, 2006. That evening, Samar had gone to comfort a friend who lost her passport which she needed to travel to college in the United States. Samar never came back. I had never written poetry before my precious child passed away, except for two poems I had written when I was eighteen years old and two more on the occasion of Omar (my son) and Qadar's (my older daughter) high school graduations. These were in Arabic. I was surprised to have written poetry and even more surprised that I did not write a poem for my third and youngest child, Samar, on her high school graduation. I remember apologizing to her on the graduation day for not writing and explaining that I had no control over the whole thing. She was most understanding and told me that I need not worry. This saddened me, however, since as a mother, I always want to treat my children equally. Who would have guessed then that I would be writing not only one or two poems for her, but several, and in two languages.

The first anniversary of my beloved daughter, Samar, passing away was approaching, and I was feeling quite miserable. I had written a poem in Arabic and planned to publish it in a local newspaper but felt frustrated at not having written anything in English on this occasion. Samar's favorite local newspaper was the main English newspaper, and I just wished that someone would publish an article or a poem for her. On August 29, 2007, I was at Bahrain's airport, waiting for my son and daughter to return from abroad, when suddenly the words of the poem *"A Year Has passed"* started pouring into my mind. I could not believe what was happening! It was this bittersweet happiness that overtook me as my wish came true and a new gift was given to me. I had this feeling that my very loved Samar was at my side, assuring me that even when I am facing the darkest of the darkest hours, some rays of light will brighten my day.

Several English poems followed; all of a sudden, I found myself spontaneously writing in both Arabic and English. Samar not only inspires me but also dictates the poem and chooses the language it should be written in. Some of my poems were written following encounters, incidents, occasions, and dreams. I feel blessed to have the ability to write and believe that God has blessed me with this gift as the anchor for the strength and stamina to survive the loss of my precious child. Poetry has come to be so pivotal for my survival; it enables me to communicate with Samar and express my feelings throughout my painful journey.

Ever since our dearest Samar passed away, I have written her a book of poetry on her birthday each year in Arabic: *Samar— Sunset and Sunrise* and *Samar, the Sun that Does Not Set*. Now, on her twenty-first birthday, this first book of poems in English, *Summer Rays*, follows the same sun theme that was so special to Samar. This title signifies the rays of inspiration that Samar brings to brighten up my dark days just like the sun's rays come through the clouds to brighten the winter days. The word Summer in the title is also important because it sounds like my daughter's name, Samar.

Samar was born on April 4, and the number four was her favorite number. Therefore, this book includes forty-four poems devoted to her with all my love. Some of these poems have been already posted on Samar's blog (www.samaralansari.com) and The Grief Blog (www.thegriefblog.com). I hope that these poems will give solace to bereaved parents and provide their loved ones with a better understanding of the pain that they live through and endure.

Randah Ribhi Hamadeh,

April 4, 2009

Acknowledgments

These poems would not have been written if my beloved Samar had not inspired me through the anguish, tears, and longing to be with her. The beautiful memories we shared during her eighteen years provoked such strong emotions, which had to flow onto paper. I am thankful to my dearest Samar for this extraordinary gift that consoles me in my profound grief.

I am most grateful to my daughter, Qadar, for her encouragement and valuable comments, which have meant so much to me. Qadar has shown tremendous emotional courage while reading my poems, feeling her pain and mine yet still being objective in her comments.

My appreciation also goes to my husband, Ahmed, and my son, Omar, for their patience while I spent many hours writing and editing my poems.

These acknowledgments would not be complete without expressing my gratitude to my parents, my siblings, and their families, as well as my friends for their support, continuous encouragement, and appreciation of my poetry. Special thanks to those supporters who read my poetry and keep track of Samar's blog.

Many thanks to all those individuals who continue to support me in my grief journey by remembering Samar, mentioning her name, and talking to me about her. I am also thankful to those friends, colleagues, family members, and others who remember

Samar's birthday, the anniversary of her passing, and other special occasions.

SAMAR

I am glad we named you SAMAR
A short name with so much power
You, darling, added to it glamour
And the scent of a special flower
With your charisma, charm, and color
A name I miss every minute and hour
I miss calling you as I call your brother
And your sister, beloved Qadar
And I yearn for your reply: "Yes, mother"
When I hear people talking to each other
Mentioning the word summer
It breaks my heart; I miss you, SAMAR

Twenty -One

Today is the day you turn twenty -one
A happy day not only for me but for everyone
But how can we celebrate it since you are gone
When your eyes cannot see the sun?

Your last birthday with us, you turned eighteen
Where are the days when you were a teen?
All these days have passed with you unseen
How do you look now? How have you been?

I wish you were here for us to celebrate
This special birthday that would change your fate
It is this year that you were supposed to graduate
I am sure you would have excelled and been great

But even though you are not here
My gift is ready for you, daughter dear
Poems of love and longing, so sincere
A special gift to mark your age this year

So here is your gift wrapped with my kisses
And all my love and special birthday wishes
Each letter, each word, your memory caresses
And tells you that you are the one everyone misses

A Year Has Passed

A broken heart, mine has become
From a pain that is only known to some

There is no pain like a mother's pain
Who is unable to see her daughter again

A year has gone, my precious one
Since you said, "Mum, come watch the sun."

Hours later, you were called to heaven above
Leaving me astounded with all those you love

No tears can wash away the grief in my heart
Your death has ripped my life apart

The amazing woman into which you have grown
Blessed with many things, let wit alone

Has been chosen to leave early by the Lord
Something that no one can prevent, young or old

Although eighteen, you left life with a mark
An older person could not have been able to spark

A remarkable young woman who no one can replace
Believe me, Samar, no one can fill your empty space

All my life for you, dear daughter, I will grieve
One year has passed, my love; do you believe?

Why Did You Come, 2008?

Why did you come, two thousand and eight?
And why is everyone happy and feeling so great?
If your intention is to bring me joy, then it is too late
Since you have already determined my fate

I cannot welcome another new year
Without having my beloved daughter near
It is amazing how everyone else wants to cheer
I guess few have lost someone so dear!

"Why are you so sad on this day?" I am asked
"Does it coincide with the day your daughter passed?
Gone should be the days that you mourn her and cry.
It is over a year since your beloved daughter died!"

Is there anyone who understands why I still cry
And don't wish another day to come and fly
And why I want to go to when my hopes were high
Two years ago, when I did not know what it is like to sigh?

Although my daughter is always in my heart, alive,
I want her next to me, when I eat, wake up, sleep, and drive.
Oh, two thousand and eight, I wish you had not arrived!
I wish you would go two New Years back and my past revive!

Eighteen Months

Eighteen months! How did I endure?
Through faith and love, that is for sure!

"Time heals" is the worst of all lies
As every part of me for her cries.

Eighteen months! without seeing her face
And without a hug or a warm embrace!

The longing grows day after day
And the heartache deepens along the way.

Eighteen months! without her beautiful smile
And without a glimpse of her profile!

She is my child, the apple of my eye
And thus, for her, everyday I yearn and cry.

Eighteen months! I have been carrying this pain
Sometimes I wonder how I managed to stay sane.

Although I am surrounded with lots of love
The fact remains that I wish her back from above.

Eighteen months! living with the empty space
A vacuum that no one can fill or replace.

So help me, Lord, to keep going along
It is only YOU who can make me strong!

Mother's Day

Mother's Day has become so incomplete
As it emphasizes your empty seat

It comes and triggers tremendous pain
As you will never celebrate it with me again

The excitement you used to have when it arrives
Remains a cherished memory all our lives

You woke up early in your special way
To wish me a Happy Mother's Day

You gave me a present that you carefully chose
And placed on my food tray a carnation or a rose

I ask the Lord to help me this day survive
The heartache that it brings since you are not alive

I am helpless and there is nothing much I can do
Except enjoy the memories I shared with you

Thank you, Lord, for the love I always get
From my children who remember and never forget

The tremendous pain that every day I am enduring
The fact that they understand is comforting and reassuring

I appreciate all the compassion and love that they give
My three are the dearest of all as long as I live

It's So Unfair

I don't think that it's fair
To celebrate my birthday
While you're not there
From life
I have already had my share
I wish, my darling, that yours
I was able to spare
To fulfill your dreams
Some of which I'm aware
What cake should I have?
What dress should I wear?
They make no sense now
As sadness fills the air
How can I survive another year?
I don't know, I swear
With a broken heart
And your empty chair
Everything around me
Is beyond repair
Sorrow and I
Are now a pair
Life truly is so unfair!

Oh, September, You Came Back Again

Oh, September, you came back again
Haven't you caused me enough pain?

Your days come and your days go
Without a glimpse of Samar and her glow.

You mark the beginning of the school year
But for me, you mark the month I lost my most dear.

Where are the days I bought her the school books
And purchased everything that suited the new year's looks?

You're back this year in Ramadan
The sacred month of the Holy Quran.

My pain will be doubled in the next days
As the memories of each rewind and play.

Oh, September, I wish you hadn't come!
Though your coming is welcomed by some.

But for me, you're the month that marks my loss
I wish our paths had never crossed!

I was told with time my pain will wane
It will not! Even when I age and walk with a cane.

Season's Greetings

As the year comes to an end,
And everyone has greetings to send,
And reserves a place for the new year to spend,
I put a smile on my face and pretend
That I am okay, as no one can fully comprehend
My heartache, neither a relative nor friend.
Forgive me, loved ones, I do not mean to offend
But my wounds will never mend
Since my grief and my blood blend.
I wish my history I could amend
And the movement of time suspend
Not having to face another year's end!

2009

How can I welcome you, 2009?
As you come without the daughter of mine
How can the stars for you shine?
When the brightest of all is with the divine
How can people go out to celebrate and dine
Drinking glasses of champagne and wine?
Tell me, how can I ever be fine
When sorrow traumatized my veins and spine
And grief embraced me and in it I am confined?
Please pardon me if I don't welcome you, 2009

Eighteen Years

Eighteen years went quickly by
Like the blink of an eye.
It's only yesterday I heard your first cry
Took you to bed and sang you a lullaby.
Comforted you when I heard you sigh,
Wiped your tears and your eyes dry.
It's only yesterday we went to buy
The several dresses you picked to try
And the eye makeup I did apply.
Your life was too short to say good-bye.
How I cherish the moments we spent,
you and I,
And miss your eyes that sparkled like
stars in the sky
And your magical smile that kept my
spirits high.
With no wings, WHY? Why did you
have to fly?

Oh, Days!

Oh, days, come back
to when we were five!
When happiness in our home
was able to thrive
The days that we enjoyed
when SAMAR was alive
The days before my beloved
went on her last drive
And before joy became
a word in our archive
Oh, present, I wish
that you had not arrived!
I never had imagined
that I would survive
a day
where in the sea of sorrow
I would dive
Oh, days, come back
to when we were five!

I'm So Sorry

Beloved mother,
I'm so sorry
I left you without a good-bye
in a hurry.
Few hours later,
you had a child to bury
and made preparations
for the obituary.
I left you
with a huge burden to carry.
I had to swiftly go,
it was involuntary.
You couldn't have stopped it,
you needn't worry.
My day had come.
Mother, I'm so sorry.

I Wish

Mother, I never imagined
you'd be standing at my grave
Praying, chatting with me
fearless and brave

Mother, I know
you are so miserable and sad
And no one can ease your pain
not even Dad

I know your happy days
with me are gone
Can a mother ever be content,
after losing a daughter or a son?

Life will forever be
to you incomplete
And joyful events
will always be bittersweet

Mother, rest assured
that I hear your cries
and listen to
your aching heart and silent sighs

I wish I could come
and wipe away your flowing tears
including the dry ones
that no one but me sees and hears

Oh, Mother, I wish
I could ease your pain

and for your sake,
bring myself back to life again

I Miss You

I cannot forget the look you had
You were so unhappy, so sad
What is it that you wanted to say?
Tell me, dear daughter, I pray!

"Mother, I miss you. Isn't it clear?
I know although I am far and near
Yet I miss throwing myself into your arms
And receiving a kiss that always calms

Although I am happy here above
I want to be with the ones I love
I miss being with my friends
Enjoying every moment, until the day ends

I miss being with my sister and brother
Watching films and laughing with one another
I miss simple things like sipping tea
And watching the sunset by the sea

Do you know now why I was about to cry?
I wish, Mother, I had stayed and did not die
I wish that we could turn back time
For these moments, I would have paid every dime

Why Did I Die?

Why are all these tears in your eyes?
Why?
I thought mothers should not cry!
They're the ones
Who keep their children's eyes dry
How ignorant was I!
A fact I can not deny
Until I left this world,
And reached the sky
And from above
Watched how much you cry
And felt your heartache
Oh, Mother!
Why did I die?

You Are a Star

Dear daughter, I hope you know
that you are a star.
When you were alive
and when you went afar.

You continue to shine
in so many people's hearts.
A star that keeps
glowing after it departs.

Precious daughter, I wish
I could bring back yesterday
to tell you
all that I wanted and yearn to say.

Although I told you,
I love you so many times
I still feel it needs
to be repeated like chimes.

You went, my darling,
without saying good-bye.
Beloved daughter,
all my life for you I will cry.

I was with you on every occasion
since you were born
and accompanied you
on each step, removing every thorn.

However, the moment you were
chosen by God to leave

I was not there with you...
for that I will always grieve.

Although I held you after
and washed you with my tears
I wish I was there then
to calm your last fears.

I talk to you
every second of my night and day
and ask the Lord
to bless you every time I pray.

I always imagined you
to be part of my tomorrow.
Instead, you left me, darling,
immersed in deep sorrow.

You Tumbled Short of Your Dreams

Daughter, you tumbled short of your dreams
Just like in the *Great Gatsby*, it seems

Did you over dream, precious child?
And your dream became unattainable and die?

And thus its attainability became very slim
An illusion replaced by a future that is so dim

I hear the recording of your warm, sweet voice
I would play it all day long if I had the choice!

You said, "If only she would walk through the door!"
Words you had uttered not realizing what was in store

"Hope never dies," you also said…
Where is the hope that one day I will see you wed?

And have three children to love and enjoy…
The dream that would have filled us all with great joy

Your dream turned out like a castle in the sand
One blow and things got out of hand

And thus your dream did not become a reality
Just as in the *Great Gatsby*, it ended in a fatality

Now it is my turn, dear daughter, not to over dream
But patiently wait to see your lovely face again beam

As you stand to welcome me at heaven's door
When my time comes to unite with you, the daughter I adore

Until then, you are alive in my heart, loved one
Even if everyone thinks that you are gone

I Carry Her in My Heart

Some people may think that I am insane
They probably have not encountered such pain

The pain of losing a daughter or a son
And knowing that from this life he or she is gone

To wake up in the morning, day after day
And ask "Where is my daughter? Tell me, I pray."

Although I know she is in heaven above
Yet I yearn to hold her and give her my love

But I also know that I carry her in my heart
We became one; no one can tear us apart

My Heart Is Broken

Although my tears
have mostly dried out…
every minute,
I cry for you and shout.

Your passing
left my heart broken
with a lot of pain,
mostly unspoken.

How can a mother's grief-
stricken heart still beat,
after seeing her loving daughter
motionless on the street?

How can a mother
see her daughter fully clad
in a snow white sheet
without feeling miserable and sad?

The wedding dress
I was hoping one day to see you in
has been replaced
by a cloth so white and thin.

I reminisce over
every happy moment we had.
And for having you
as my daughter, I am so glad.

I am so fortunate
to be your mother

and so are your father,
sister, and brother.

You have made us
all very proud
as you are remembered
by everyone all year round.

If it was not for the love
and memories you left behind
I would have been buried by now,
next to you in the sand.

Days Are Not the Same

Days come and days go…
but they have lost
their glamour and glow
And become empty
… full of awe
since we had our biggest blow.

Days are dull and not the same…
how can I go on
without calling your name?
And without seeing you,
a beautiful dame?
Alas! All that I have now
are pictures in a frame.

No heart is bigger
than a mother's heart
But can I forgive life
… which pulled us apart?
Although I am thankful to God,
there is no doubt.
Yet my heart bleeds
since you departed.

With every glance,
I see you there
like my shadow,
following me everywhere.
Or as an angel
who hears my prayer
and comes to comfort me,
by just being there.

The Incomplete

There is no joy
With the start of a new day
Things are incomplete
No matter what you say
My daughter is gone
Oh God, why did I have to stay?
I should have gone before her!
She should have been alive today
This is what I learned
As the rules of the play

How can a mother
Outlive her child?
It is something unimaginable
Beyond anybody's mind.
My family is incomplete
Since my daughter died
And my tears cannot bring her back
No matter how much I cry
How can life ever be the same
When she is on the other side?

This loss is the ultimate loss
That no one can describe
With no limit to its grief
No line to circumscribe
There is no medicine for it
That doctors can prescribe
It is engraved in the mother's eyes,
No need for anyone to inscribe
"Loss of a child," no language
Will ever be able to transcribe

Going to Places

Going to places has not been fun
Since the moment you were gone.

I try hard to put a smile on my face
And hide the pain that I within embrace.

But still I am asked, "Why are your eyes so sad?"
"Do you have any worries or did your day go bad?"

Or they might ask, "Are you not well?"
What shall I answer? "I am going through hell."

Suppose I say, "For my beloved daughter I grieve."
They will be in shock, I believe.

I try very hard to get along
And show the world that I am fine and strong.

But the plight that I have faced
Is engraved in my face and cannot be erased.

So listen, stranger, do not venture and ask
It is better for you that I keep the mask.

The happiness that I once enjoyed
In going to places is gone, leaving me void.

Little Bo Peep

I closed my eyes
trying to get some sleep
Unsuccessful
even after I counted all the sheep
And after going over
the memories I treasure and keep
So I held my beloved's picture
and started to weep
Oh pain!
you have grown inside me so deep
The path of grief is long and steep
Where is the future
that she was supposed to reap?
Oh longing for my daughter
every moment, you creep
And keep me awake
when the world around me is asleep
Oh Lord, let me doze
and have a glimpse of her or a peep
In a dream as when
she happily drove the Jeep
Or when she was running
or hearing her phone beep
Or when she was a child
and I sang for her "Little Bo Peep"
For without a glance of her
I can no longer this life upkeep

If You Had One More Day

Daughter, if you had one more day
And the Lord allowed you to stay

I would have…
Kept you in my arms
And kissed you more than a thousand times

I would have…
Told you, "You make me proud"
And shouted "I LOVE YOU" out loud

I would have…
Thanked you for every little thing
And the abundant joy you used to bring

I would have…
Told you how thoughtful you are
To watch over everyone from heaven, like a star

I would have…
Apologized for causing you any dismay
While disciplining or during fun and play

I would have…
Given you one more hug
And made your special tea in your favorite mug

I would have…
Asked you to say "Mama" again and again
So that your voice gets embossed in my brain

I would have…
Gone with you for one more ride
And bought you a special dress, that of a bride

I would have…
Accompanied you to the places you'll miss
Places you loved, which witnessed your bliss

I would have…
Gathered all your friends
To embrace you with happiness till the day ends

I would have…
Baked your favorite apple pie
And pleaded to God to spare you and instead I die
If only you had one more day
We could have said good-bye in a proper way

Can You Take Away My Endless Pain?

Can you take away my endless pain?
Then stop preaching! Your plea is in vain.

"It is good to do this or do that," you comment.
"Get closure and move on and stop your lament."

These words make my heart ache.
Please, do not mention them, for my sake.

I know your intention is to comfort me.
However, you are causing me pain, can't you see?

Time is the best healer everyone says.
It will get better and easier throughout the days.

You do not understand; it is a shame!
Believe me, I know it is out of love; there is no blame.

Is it a page in a book that I can turn?
Or an incense stick that I can burn?

There are no seasons for my grief
My tears will keep pouring without relief.

Even though her physical presence is no more
I know that she is with me, the daughter I adore.

I hope that no mother would have to endure
The heartache that neither time nor words could ever cure.

Why Are You Not Moving On?

I'm asked, "Why are you not moving on?
It's been over a year since your daughter has gone!"

These words hurt me and tear me apart.
There is no end to the grief in my heart!

"Your tomorrow will soon be filled with joy
When you have a grandchild, a girl or a boy."

It's very hard to feel that you are suddenly alone
As others don't wish to continue hearing you groan.

Try to understand me, friends and loved ones
As you all have daughters and sons.

And try to accept the person I became
Since the one you love will never be the same.

I don't see at times when I open my eyes.
This is what happens when a daughter dies.

I'll never be able to spend a single night or day
Without talking about my daughter or for her praying.

I know that for you, she and I are so dear.
Be assured that to me this is crystal clear.

I'm sure that my well -being is your concern
But please realize that every minute for her, I yearn.

Don't Ask Me

"Remove her pictures
and to her grave don't go.
Empty her room,
you'll feel better, I know

Because as long as you cling
to every thing
sadness will always
at your door bell ring."

Your words
are breaking my heart.
You want me to forget
what is of me a part?

Now my beloved
is closer to me than before
I keep her in my heart
and close the door

Leave me alone
in the way I handle my grief
My heartache
is severe beyond belief

The ultimate loss of a child
is so unique
It will never ease
but makes the parent weak

And the mother's grief
so profound

It gets deeper and deeper
as the years go round

So please don't ask me
not to do this or that
But give me a hug
and about her let's chat

How Many Children?

"How many children do you have?" I am asked
My answer to them will never be masked

I have a boy and two girls, a total of three
Two on earth and one whose soul has gone free

Two my hand can reach and embrace
And one left us all with an empty space

She was so eager to meet the Lord
Perhaps, from this senseless life, she got bored

The person is speechless and in shock
It seems like I have hit her with a rock

But what else can I answer, if I may ask?
To make it easier on people is a difficult task!

"But you have two then, am I right?"
No! I have three even though she is out of sight

Don't you count your child when he is away?
Then why are you so surprised, if I may say?

Didn't I carry all the three in my womb
And in my life and heart gave each one equal room?

Then how can I now this fact deny
To save you the shock? Do you want me to lie?

Men Can Cry

I want you to know
that men can cry
They shouldn't hold their tears
when loved ones die

And if the deceased
is someone so dear
Don't be so scared
to drop a tear

I assure you
that I feel your pain
Tell me what good it does
if silent you remain?

Instead, be yourself
and express your sorrow
Shed your tears
and in your grief wallow

Shout, scream
and call up her name
Even though
society considers it a shame

A Mother's Grief

"In time, dear, your wound will heal
And you'll observe changes in how you feel
Your suffering will lessen a great deal"
Words said to comfort but so unreal

Words that bring tears to a mother's eyes
She is hurt but they don't realize
What the loss of a child does even to the wise
A part of her is gone when a child dies.

Bereaved mothers are unique in their grief
Their bereavement is for life, not short and brief
Lamenting a child is endless, without any relief
Believe me, they aren't in denial or disbelief

Accept their sorrow and endless pain
Their ultimate loss is of no return
Thank God they survived it and are still sane
Allow them to grieve without any restraint

Acknowledge that a mother's heart will never heal
Understand what she goes through and feels
Try to be less demanding of her is my appeal
And don't ask her to bury her sorrow and conceal

You Will Heal

Words of advice like
"You will heal"
To a grieving mother
are so unreal.
Is her heart
made of steel?
Or of layers
that she can peel?
Grief to mothers
is like a spinning wheel.
No one can appreciate the pain
she feels
Or the agony
that is felt
and she conceals.
Do not advise a grieving mother
I appeal
And tell her that one day
"You will heal."

For Those I Left Behind

For those of you I left behind
I know that I am in everyone's mind

You remember me in your own way
Every minute of the day

You remember me with each sunrise
And when the sun sets and the sky cries

Whenever you take a car ride
On the empty seat, I sit and hide

And when you go to a place I like
I walk with you on my invisible bike

And when you eat my favorite food
It will boost up your low mood

Rest assured that I hear your prayer
You do not see me, but I am always there

I Am Not Walking Alone

Beloved daughter, rest assured
that I am not walking alone
Many are grieving for you
with feelings explicitly shown
While others prefer to be private
and in silence cry and moan
I now realize more than ever
Gibran's words
"Your children are not your own"
Words engraved in my mind
now as well as in stone
The meaning of which
I hardly realized
the day you were born
I am not alone
when I cry for you
at the early hours of the dawn
As someone else
is surely calling your name
in a different time zone
It is incredible how many hearts
ache for you and mourn
as you are the most amazing person
they have ever known
and the kindest of the girls
with whom they had grown
I wish that you knew how much
love towards me had blown
and that I was approached by many
even the withdrawn

to tell me how much they miss you
since you have flown
and the many times they wished
to talk to you and call your phone
Expecting a miracle!
To hear your sweet voice
with its unique tone
So rest assured, beloved daughter
that I am not walking alone

You and I

How much I enjoyed
our being alone,
just you and I!
My beloved daughter,
friend, companion, and ally.
The special time we had,
I'll cherish until I die.
The silence, talks, walks
and memories made time fly.
I wish the moment hadn't arrived
for us to say good-bye.
I'll miss
your look of understanding
into my eye
that says, "Mother,
it's okay to cry.
You're yearning for my sister,
your looks imply.
You're doing your best,
I know how much you try
to hide your pain
and conceal a tear or a sigh.
Beloved mother,
for that don't feel at all shy.
Allow me to share your thoughts
and your tears dry
for when I was a child,
you sang me a song or a lullaby
and comforted me
when my fears
were about to intensify.
Now it's my turn

to ease your pain even if I
have to get you
a piece of the sky.
Rest assured, dear mother,
my sister didn't die.
I see her alive in you,
a fact that I can't deny."

Dear Nieces

Dear nieces,

I know how much you try
To hold your tears and not cry.

I feel the sadness that you try to hide
And the heartache you keep deep inside.

In our looks, her memory we embrace
And we see her in each other's faces.

I am writing this to let you know
That I recognize the pain you try not to show.

I want to thank you and express my love
Along with that sent to you from heaven above.

Thank You, Friend

Thank you, friend, for always being there for me
And seeing what I saw and did not see

I am blessed to have you by my side
In good times, bad times, and when I lost my child

You have accepted the person I became
And realized that your friend can not be the same!

Friend, you have never asked me to change
And never considered any of my behaviors strange

You have decided to walk with me at my pace
And understood that no one can take Samar's place

You respected my daily sorrow and tears
And appreciated my strength in facing my loss and fears

You wished me patience and serenity of the soul
And prayed that God helps me survive living with my hole

You even joined me in appreciating the sunrise
This significant act, dear friend, is not a surprise!

Although the burden you carry is not small
You never shy away from listening to me, not at all

Thank you for always tolerating my talk
About my beloved Samar, since the days she started to walk

Although seeing me immersed in grief is painful to you
You are always there for me, the friend I knew

With you, dear friend, I will always feel free
To talk about my loss at any stage or degree

I am grateful that you do not push me to move along
And acknowledge my pain and listen to my song

Thank you, dear friend, for all the support
And God bless you for the comfort you brought

Could That Have Been You?

The dream was so vivid
beyond belief
It was very meaningful
although it was brief
A little girl appeared
and commented on my grief
gave me a big hug
and words of relief

She told me that her family
visits the blog everyday
and reads everything I post
and appreciates what I say:
"We are sad for you
and for you we all pray
Oh, bereaved mother!
I wish your days were not so gray."

Beloved daughter,
could that little girl have been you?
Holding my hand
and comforting me as you used to do
The resemblance was great
the differences very few
How can I interpret the dream otherwise?
I have no clue!

So you came in a dream
to console my aching heart
to tell me that you're with me

Even death can't split us apart
And that you're watching
what I am doing from the start
Oh, my angel
from my life you'll never depart!

I Look for You

I look for you all around and find you
Everywhere, in every corner, in every place
We had memories to share. I look for you
Yet my heart tells me Stop searching,
You and your beloved daughter are now a pair
Your love and faith keep her alive. Close your eyes
And you will see her beautiful smile and black hair
And you will smell her special fragrant scent in the air

She is an angel needed in heaven to look after you and care

Never Died

I find myself alive every moment of the day
Mother, is this what happens to the dead, I pray?

I am alive in your heartbeat
And in the blood that flows from your head to feet.

Oh, Mother, even though I am out of sight
You made my image so clear and bright.

There are many "alive" as they say
But no one mentions them every day.

As for me, I am very satisfied
That you make it seem like I never died.

Hello from Heaven

Beloved mother, as you fly
today in the sky up high
You'll feel my presence
no need to ask how or why
I'm here to comfort you
as you'll miss me and cry
And shed your tears
of them, you never shy
But look at the window
and your eyes will surely dry
As I come with the sunrise
to greet you as you fly
And embrace you with
my love from the sky
A warm hello from heaven
mother, I didn't die
Speak to me! I can hear
even if I don't reply
As between you and me
there is never a good-bye

Please, Mother, Don't Cry

Please, Mother, Don't Cry
When you miss me, look at the sky
You'll find me shining with the stars up high
When the sun rises and sets, I greet you with a hello or hi
And with the birds I send you messages as they fly
Each morning I hug you and kiss each eye

Please, Mother, Don't Cry
I'm with you, a fact that no one can deny
You'll smell me in a rose or jasmine that you buy
And you'll hear me in a song or a lullaby
And see me in the faces of any girl or guy
Smile, Mother. I am free now like a butterfly

Please, Mother, Don't Cry
Your face has changed, I can hardly identify
You've withered. I don't need to ask why
You call my name but there is no reply
Happiness is gone, you can't get or buy
Mother, rest assured I'm with you, by your side I lie

My Most Dear

I know you recognize me,
my most dear
When I whisper "I love you"
in your ear
In a soundless voice
that you can hear
And when I wipe from your face
every tear
And steal a kiss so warm
and sincere
To others, I am gone
it might appear
But for you,
to your heart and mind I adhere
Mother, my physical absence
do not fear
I am always with you,
I did not disappear
Although I am very far,
yet I am so near

You'll Find Me

Mother, look around you,
you'll find me…
When you look at the mirror,
you'll find me…
In the faces of my siblings,
you'll find me…
When you are with my friends,
you'll find me…
In the empty seats,
you'll find me…
When you watch the sunrise,
you'll find me…
And as the sun sets,
you'll find me…
As you look at the sea,
you'll find me…
And in the desert sands,
you'll find me…
With the beauty of flowers,
you'll find me…
Mother, wherever you look,
you'll find me.

About the Author

Randah Ribhi Hamadeh is a wife, mother, and professor in Family and Community Medicine, College of Medicine and Medical Sciences, Arabian Gulf University, Bahrain. She received her doctorate (DPhil) in epidemiology from the University of Oxford. The author of several professional papers, she has also published two collections of poetry in Arabic. Please visit her blog: www.samaralansari.com. She can be contacted at randahhamadeh@hotmail.com.